BLACK WHITENESS

Admiral Byrd Alone in the Antarctic

by Robert Burleigh

illustrated by Walter Lyon Krudop

ATHENEUM BOOKS FOR YOUNG READERS

THE GENERAL INFORMATION FOR THIS BOOK COMES MAINLY FROM *ALONE* BY RICHARD BYRD, PUBLISHED BY INTERNATIONAL COLLECTOR LIBRARY, GARDEN CITY, NEW YORK, 1938.

Atheneum Books for Young Readers
An imprint of Simon & Schuster Children's Publishing Division
1230 Avenue of the Americas
New York, New York 10020

Book design by Patti Ratchford
The text of this book is set in Minion
The illustrations are rendered in oil and vinyl paint.

First Edition
Printed in Hong Kong by South China Printing Co. (1988) Ltd.
10 9 8 7 6 5 4 3 2 1

Library of Congress Cataloging-in-Publication Data
Black whiteness / by Robert Burleigh ; illustrated by Walter Lyon Krudop.—1st ed.
p. cm.
Summary: An account of Admiral Richard Byrd's stay alone in a small shack during an Antarctic winter.
ISBN 978-1-4424-5334-0
1. Byrd, Richard Evelyn, 1888–1957—Juvenile literature. 2. Antarctica—Discovery and exploration—Juvenile literature. 3. Explorers—United States—Biography—Juvenile literature.
[1. Byrd, Richard Evelyn, 1888–1957. 2. Explorers. 3. Antarctica—Discovery and exploration.]
I. Krudop, Walter, 1966, ill. II. Title.
G585.B8B87   1998
919.8'904—dc20
96-21999   CIP   AC

For Stuart McCarrell, with many thanks.
—R. B.

To the Byrd Polar Research Center and The Explorers
Club, many thanks.
—W. K.

Antarctica. March 1934.
A man stands alone in the snow,
watching a tractor disappear over the far horizon.

Wherever he turns now,
he sees the flat whiteness roll on forever to meet the sky;
he feels the things of the world "shrink away to nothing."

It is midafternoon,
but the sun to the south is already setting.
Night is coming on,
pressing down with its blue-black shadow.

He kneels and opens a small hatch.

Below, buried like a cave in the snow,

is the tiny shack where he will live alone for many months.

He puts his foot on the first rung of the ladder and lowers

himself inside.

Admiral Richard Byrd, explorer, moves about his snug house,
"tidily built as a watch."
With four strides, he can cross the room:
past the bunk on a wall, a stove, shelves, hooks for clothes.

His narrow world is a dim one, too:
He has only a flashlight, a lantern, and a small gas lamp.
There are three thin windows in the roof;
the ceiling is made of aluminum
to reflect what little light there is.

Outside the door is a kind of porch.
The ladder to the hatch rests on it.
Leading away are two long, low tunnels.
It is here that he stores his tons of fuel and food.
His toilet is a hole at the end of one of the tunnels,
thirty-five feet away.

The tunnels are dark as dungeons. But in the lantern light, they take on a breathless radiance. Icicles on the roof glisten like candelabra; the walls glow with a sharp, blue nakedness.

Advance Base is the first inland base in Antarctica.
There are eight weather instruments,
and each day Byrd must record the information they give.
The instruments tell the wind's speed and direction.
They tell the temperature.
They tell the amount of moisture in the air.
Scientists around the world want to know these things.

But Admiral Byrd wants to know something else, too.
What is it like to live so completely alone?
In such intense cold and so much darkness?
Can any human being endure that?
Can he—Richard Byrd?

He keeps a diary where, at the end of each day,
he writes down his thoughts.
Writing like this, he tells himself, is like "thinking out loud."

Out here, in frost and darkness as complete as that of the Ice Age, I may have time to catch up, to study, and to think. I am able to live exactly as I choose, obedient to nothing but the laws of the wind and the night and the cold. That is the way I see it.

Little America, the main base, is many miles away on the
    Antarctic coast.
Admiral Byrd contacts the people at Little America on
    his radio.
He can hear their voices,
but he can only reply in a code of dashes and dots.

The rest is mostly an eerie silence—
except for the constant ticking of the weather machines,
and the ceaseless blowing of the wind.

Cold, terrible cold:

At −50°F a flashlight dies in his hand;
at −55°F kerosene freezes;
at −60°F rubber turns brittle and snaps,
juice bottles shatter,
canned food from the tunnel becomes hard as rock.
Outside, he hears his breath freeze as it floats away,
making a sound like firecrackers.
Sometimes the frozen breath hangs above his head like
    a small cloud;
if he breathes too deeply, his lungs burn with invisible fire.

There is also a terrible beauty:
afternoon skies that shatter "like broken goblets"
as tiny ice crystals fall across the face of the sun;
blood-red horizons, liquid twilights,
and pale green beams, called auroras,
that wind in great waves through the towering dark.

But it is April now,
and "each day more light is draining away."
Soon there will be no sun at all.
Days and days and days of total blackness.
The Antarctic night.

With two weeks of daylight left, the sun was just a monstrous ball which could barely hoist itself free of the horizon. It would sink out of sight in the north not long after noon. I watched it go as one might watch a departing friend.

Mornings are the worst.
The cold in the little room lies like a thick liquid.
This morning, in the shack, it is –40°F!
(He sleeps with the stove off and the door half open,
in order to be safe from any possible fumes.)

The slightest move sends blasts
of freezing air down his back or stomach.
The thought of his first foot on the floor makes him cringe.

Ice coats the outside of the sleeping bag.
His clothes are so stiff
he must work them between his hands
    before putting them on.

He pokes with the flashlight
to find a pair of thin silk gloves.
Without the gloves,
the frozen metal of the lantern would
    tear skin off his fingers!

He strikes a match and touches it to the lantern's wick.
The flame catches and goes out,
catches and goes out.
Then it wavers, steadies, thickens:
ah, light!

It is a gloomy light perhaps; things on the opposite wall are scarcely touched by it. But to me the feeble burning is a daily miracle.

In this cruel world, even the simple is difficult.
The snow is rough and brittle as white sandstone.
He cuts out blocks with a saw,
then melts them in a bucket on the stove, slowly:
after several hours over the flame,
two gallons of snow make two quarts of water.

Sometimes, as he opens the trapdoor,
the wind sweeps down
and sucks all the heat from the house.

At the close of each day, standing by the stove,
he bathes a third of his body.
(Because warm air rises and cool air sinks,
it is often 20° colder at his feet!)

Finally, with all heat off,
he reads in the sleeping bag—until his hands are numb.

Patiently, he parcels out the day:
checks each instrument many times;
writes out and stores his reports;
patches the stovepipe;
observes the sky at intervals and notes down whatever he sees.
(He calls his observations "obs.")

Each afternoon he takes a long walk.
But in the black whiteness of the Antarctic winter,
he is never quite safe or sure.

One day he walks out beyond his trail
marked by bamboo sticks
and realizes he is lost.
He panics, and almost starts to run;
then calms himself and once more finds his way.

On another day he stumbles over a small hole.
Crawling carefully to the edge,
he points his flashlight, leans, and looks down—
into a deep crevasse!

At the surface the crevasse was not more than three feet across; but a little way down it bellied out, making a vast cave. I could see no bottom.

Blizzard.

Like an incoming tide, the snow rises:
over his ankles,
above his knees,
against his chest,
exploding into his eyes
"like millions of tiny pellets."

No night has ever seemed so dark.
The flashlight's beam blackens.
The trapdoor, weighted by the sudden snow,
is stuck tight.

Terrified, Byrd rips and claws at the hatch-edge.

You are reduced to a crawling thing on the margin of
a disintegrating world.

The drift piles up around him.
The air comes at him in white rushes.
If he tries to stand,
the snow wall beats him back.

He stabs at the hatch with his shovel.
Again and again and again.
He pries open an inch, forces in his fingers,
hauls it up high and higher;
and, moaning, tumbles inside.

Late May.
And suddenly,
what he had feared the most happens.

Gas fumes seep into one of the tunnels!
Carbon monoxide, odorless and invisible.

Unknowing, Byrd walks into the tunnel
and leans over the radio.
He feels a strange drowsiness.
His eyes flutter.
His legs grow weak.
He falls to his hands and knees on the icy floor.
He does not remember turning the radio off,
nor crawling back toward the shack,
nor butting the door open like a wounded animal.

All he would ever remember was the "skyrocketing pain,"
the violent beating of his heart,
and a voice inside him saying, *I must sleep.*

Only the cold was real: the numbness in the hands
and feet, creeping like a slow paralysis through
my body. I grasped for the throat of the sleeping bag,
and eased in.

He wakes at last, deathly sick.
With trembling hands,
he lights the candle above his bed.

When he stands on his quivery legs, he feels pain and nausea.
Intense hunger.
Dreadful thirst.
He nibbles on a small piece of chocolate;
he sucks on slivers of ice
until his teeth rattle from the cold.

The candle casts its heatless, gloomy light
into the corners of the shack.
Admiral Byrd crawls back into the bag and lies there,
composing last letters to his loved ones in America.

There is no hope, he thinks, *no hope.*
I am going to die.

The days pass in a blur of broken images.
Yet something in him fights to stay alive.
He manages to light the stove.
He eats a little.

But his strength is gone.
He does not stand—he wobbles.
He does not walk—he creeps.

Getting fuel from the tunnel is a morning's work.
Climbing the ladder to go "topside,"
he stops to rest at every rung.

Outside or inside, day or night,
he is cold to his very bones.

Talking with Little America is harder, too.

He cranks the radio by hand.
"The room at –60°, sweat pouring down my chest."

Should he say he is sick?

That he is going to die?

No, an attempt to rescue him would only doom the men.

I had given a hard and fast order not to come for me until a month after the sun returns.

Do the people at Little America,

receiving his slow, misspelled replies,

know he is not well?

Noon. June 21:
the longest night of the Antarctic year.

Richard Byrd sits in the snow, staring out.
Darkness on three sides.
But in the north there is a faint dab of crimson on the
distant horizon;
a thin pencil line of light,
like a secret message from the now-returning sun.
But beyond the weather records
(which he keeps up day after day)
he is too weak to write,
too despairing to see.

In his struggle to stay alive,

all else falls away.

Uneaten food litters the floor.

Half-empty cans are flung out on the deck.

Frozen slop is dumped in the tunnels.

Spare parts are scattered about like ice chunks.

Books lie underneath their shelves,

their upthrust pages stiff as frozen sails.

A small mirror hangs on the wall.

He gazes into it.

He leans close, listens,

and thinks he hears a very tiny voice:

Endure, it says;

Live, it says.

July is "born in cold."

(Twenty days will be colder than 60° below!)

Yet a message arrives from Little America:

A tractor team is coming—sooner than planned.

Is it possible?

A human face again?

A living voice?

Outside, the air rains with an unbelievable coldness.

Ice crystals

burn as they fall on his skin,

cling to his eyelashes,

sealing his eyes half shut.

My toes would turn cold and then dead. While I
danced up and down to restore the circulation, my
nose would freeze; by the time I attended to that, my
hand was frozen.

Inside, "nothing is left for the ice to conquer":

It covers the floor;

it climbs up the walls;

it curves around the vent pipe;

it crawls across the ceiling.

On the table in the middle of the room,

a piece of meat lies unthawed.

It has been there for five days.

The tractor has set out twice,
and twice been forced to turn back.
Yesterday it started again.
(It will take two full days to arrive.)
He hears this on his radio,
but what he hears means less and less:
he has ceased to believe it is coming;
he has almost ceased to care.

In the gloom, he thinks of the tractor men.
Will *they* survive?
He imagines them wandering past, beeping beyond him,
lost in the endless dark;
he imagines them tumbling down snow hills,
blinded by the white wind.

With his feeble arms, he painfully pushes himself up.
Yes, there is something he can—he must—do.
His thoughts search among the tunnel's rubble.
For a moment, he feels new blood course through his
    tired veins.
In his mind, he begins to make a plan.

Suddenly, I had a task to do.
My job would be that of a lighthouse keeper
on a dangerous coast.

August 10:
a night "black with threat."

Byrd stands by the open hatch,
hauling a T-shaped kite upward by a thin string.
Around its long wire tail are wads of paper and pieces of cloth.
He douses the kite's tail with gasoline,
and tries to light a match.
A dozen matches go out in his hand.

Finally, a violent uprush of light almost blinds him.
He jerks on the kite string.
The kite swoops into the air, caught on a wind gust,
flapping its spidery tail, blazing against the black.
It rises and rises, skates to a height of over a hundred feet.

The sight of it swaying in the night sky delights him.
This beacon, he knows, can be seen for miles and miles.

For five minutes the kite flames overhead.
Byrd squints. He blinks and peers northward.

Against the backdrop of the horizon,
a single fingery beam moves up and down.
Afraid to believe it is true, he turns away,
shuts his two eyes tight and waits.
Then he turns and looks again.

There it is, still poking at the dark!
Quickly, he lights a flare and ties it to a stick.
He holds the stick high, waving it wildly.
The flare makes "a huge blue hole in the night."

The light from the tractor grows and grows.
Treads crunch over the crusted snow.
Horns sound and the tractor stops.
Three fur-muffled figures leap out.

Byrd wants to stay calm,
but his hands are shaking.
He wants to cry,
but he is too empty even to sob.

He tries to jest: "Come on below, boys,
I have bowls of hot soup waiting."

Then, following the men down the ladder,
he collapses on the porch.

Many weeks pass.
The men from Little America help Admiral Byrd
    regain his strength.
They chart the weather, cook, clean,
sleep on the floor.

The darkness lifted from my heart, just as it presently
did from the Barrier.

At last, the Antarctic spring arrives
with a great blossoming of light.
One morning Admiral Byrd climbs
up the ladder and out the hatch.
He walks slowly across the snow,
to a small airplane waiting for him.
As the plane rises into the brightening air,
he looks down at the roof of his little house for the final time.

Admiral Richard Byrd will return to Antarctica.
He will tell the people of the world more
about this beautiful but harsh continent.

He will also write a book about his time alone.
He will talk about the cold and the fear and the courage.
But most of all he will tell about
"the sheer beauty and miracle of being alive."

"I live more simply now," he writes at the end of his book,
"and with more peace."